Collection Of A Novice Wordsmith

Tanishq Kalra

Copyright © 2024 Tanishq Kalra

Made with ❤ on the Notion Press Platform

www.notionpress.com

For all the novice wordsmiths who craft their worlds through words.
For all the readers who find their worlds within them

Chapters

Whispers In English

While reading heavenly pieces
of other artisans' wordsmithery,
my heart melts and my soul freezes.
Yet my mind ponders how they
have been written,
though I am irritated,
lava inside my mind boils reading these,
and soon an eruption will occur.
I will call it an eruption of gigantic melodies,
which will release a storm in reader's hearts
thereafter,
my soul will freeze and my heart will melt
while reading my heavenly pieces.

I want people to remember my poems,
I want them to feel attached.
I want my diary to get dirty in cosmic dust,
I want my ink to be meteorically dispatched.

Every day I have new aspirations to write,
every day I find something new.
Sometimes it's a roaring sun behind the clouds,
sometimes it's lunar whispers of the moon.

I write because I'm in love. No
I write because it gives me tranquility.
I write because my heart is broken. No
I write because penning whispers of the mind is my
favorite activity.

But does it make me happy?
Now, this question is an infinite loop.
But happiness is a practice, right?
With this question, we are all duped.

When I was small and was playing with a dart,
I dreamed of a bunny to fill my heart.
In my youth, dreams were grand,
I prayed for cars and money in my hand.
As time passed away old dreams faded,
wishing for big homes and millions each day.
In my early teens prayed for something truly rare,
a good look and a pretty smile to share.
Now I dream of peace and prosperity,
not just earning, but embracing charity.
No need for big homes and millions, in a world
rearranged,
Growing up, my prayers beautifully changed.

Don't use wood in his cremation;
he wants to burn in his books,
The books that he wrote,
the books which belong to him.

He wants his words
to disappear with him.
He wants his poetry
to become ashes with him.

He wants his fiction
to be fictional with him.
He wants his writings
to only be with him.

Yet he will be the best,
yet he will be remembered.
His books will become ashes,
but his legacy will be remembered.

They did a debate, Who?
Devastating sky and gigantic sea.
The heavens whispered down
to the water, "Let us go far and see
which is more spread.
Whether it's you or it's me"

Thousands of kilometers both
enjoying, Thereafter
a shore reaches out to embrace the sea.
Sky said, "I am vast, Hence powerful.
You have to agree."

"Your expanse exceeds my shores,
but the depth I hold
surpasses your height, moreover
I can demolish Earth through
the flow of my tide,"
Sea swiftly echoed.

Blue Sky chuckled and retorted,
"I hold the moon, which Reigns
supreme over your cute waves.
You and your tide,
are but pawns To the power I employ."

I am in love with the sun,
during sunset, he said,
"We'll see each other next morning,
I am loyal, I promise."
In the night, I saw the moon,
radiant and shining bright.
The moon was beautiful,
I fell in love at first sight.
Spent the night with moon,
gazed by its light.
I was staring at it
all through the night.
As the sun was rising,
the moon started to disappear.
Sun was rising rapidly,
as if it wanted to eagerly appear.
The sun said to me, "Look, I am back."
I replied, "Yes! Please stay disappeared the whole night
and come every morning like this."
How can I be this selfish?

The chessboard is your life,
every step you take matters a lot.
Black is your enemy,
and you are in your white fort.

Where self-doubt is their king
and your biggest enemy.
Adversity, the queen of black,
weakens you mentally.

Small tests on your way,
like pawns in a row.
And you're the king,
with your queen beside,

Bishop is your faith,
resilience the rook,
confidence is the pawn, pick that up,
and make your move.

Be confident and you'll
always find a way to win.
The chessboard is your life,
let the battle begin.

Because of death, life is devitable.
Because of life, death is inevitable.

Love is freedom, Love is restriction
Love can be broken, But love isn't perfection

Love is avoidance, Love is an addiction
Love brings happiness, But love isn't destruction

Love is a sacrifice, Love is a feeling
Love is a pain, Love is a healing

Love is ugly, Love is appealing
Sometimes it's everywhere
Sometimes it's concealing

Holding an umbrella with that slow walk,
It was the first time
when I saw you and wanted to talk.

Your beautiful smile made me sane,
It was the first time
I chased a girl to see her again.

One day while reading a book, you were sitting on the
grass,
It was the first time
To see you, I didn't attend my class.

I gathered my confidence to approach, so I walked,
It was the first time
You saw me, and we talked.

That evening our eyes met, stars above,
It was the first time
I felt like, I was in love.

Yes, I know you hate me, but I can't.
What should I do now?
Is my heart safe with you?
I guess not; it is shattered somehow.
Well, that's not unexpected.
You should have told me before
rather than leaving now.
You made my days heaven earlier
and now making them hell somehow
Thanks a lot for this gift, darling.
I will not be the same person now.

One just whispers
for help,
everyone listens
his slow yelp.

Another shouted
in the crowd.
Everyone ignored
his loud.

Why did this happen?
I ponder.
Karma is the one
behind these wonders.

Are you not well?
Or is it just your brain playing a game?
Why does it feel like hell?
Or are your actions to blame?
Why so much frustration?
Or does everyone experience the same?
Why so much stress?
Or is it all about the overthinking game?
Why is peace leaving you?
Or is it just you, not knowing how to claim.

There is an ambition, far from comfort,
calling for a meet, but there is a condition,
I have to suffer.
I know the weather of the journey is bad,
and I have to prepare myself for that.
To just follow my ambition, I put myself in trouble.
The journey was difficult; I was unaware of this
struggle.
I achieved it. Now, what's the award?
You follow your ambition—This itself is a reward.

I saw you yesterday with your friends,
You looked stunning.
When you tucked your hair behind your ear,
There I saw, in your smile, a silver sheen coming.
You looked at me and took my breath away,
And I loved that, so please do that again, today.
Trap me again in those beautiful eyes,
If I feel like I am buzzed, I won't be surprised.
मैं आज फिर तुझे देखूंगा
तू आज फिर से एक फरिश्ता लगेगी
गलती से नज़रें मिल जाएं तुझसे अगर
मुझे तू फिर से एक जादुई हसीना लगेगी
Talking about you is pure fantasy,
Not going to lie, your beauty has left a legacy.
Whispering to God that I want you,
I want you so, I want your charming symphony.

Tales Untold

The Boon Of Eternity

This penthouse will cost you around six and a half crore." The builder asserted with firm confidence. Without much negotiation, Rahul made the advance payment and bought that penthouse.

Rahul was a serial entrepreneur, his recent startup was bootstrapped and sold to Ola Electric for $15 million, his startup was about making batteries for electric vehicles. He was married to Arpita and they had a son, Anshul. Anshul was studying in the US, a rich kid, old hat. Arpita was a software engineer who worked in Rahul's startup.

Arpita was recently diagnosed with cancer, the only regrettable matter in this family. Rahul wanted to buy a penthouse to spend precious moments with his wife, as their son was abroad and they were a secluded couple.

A swimming pool, lofty ceiling, astonishing woodwork, beautiful view from the 25th floor, and whatnot. This penthouse was stunningly gorgeous, but one thing on the roof ended up being a fly in the ointment—an unshakable small round rusted container.

Rahul and his workers tried to move the container, but couldn't. It seemed as if it had a concrete pillar attached to the earth. Rahul called the builder to know the mystery of this container, to which the builder replied, "Sir, it was here since the building was made, and it doesn't matter. It's merely a small container." Rahul was convinced, but little did he know how mighty that container was.

One night, a strong thunderstorm hit the city, with high decibels of lightning sound and heavy rain. Both couples were sleeping when, all of a sudden, they heard a booming sound. It wasn't lightning; it came from the terrace. Rahul took his umbrella and went up to check what had happened.

When he opened the door of the terrace, he sensed the odor of an explosion. He went outside and was dumbfounded. The rusted container had exploded, and its iron pieces were spread out on the terrace. He carefully went near the place where the container was placed and observed a glass bottle there. Cautiously picking up the bottle, he was returning when he slipped. The bottle and umbrella dropped from his hand, and a massive ten-foot-blue man appeared. Rahul gazed at this giant, the odor of explosion replaced by a pleasant fragrance coming from the genie.

Rahul fearfully asked, "Are you a Genie?" The genie inspected him, rolled his eyes, and replied, "I guess so." Rahul's eyes were wide open, frightened by this giant. To make Rahul believe he was a real genie, the genie snapped his finger, and the next moment, they were both in the gym, and Rahul was dried. "Did you believe?" the genie smirked. Rahul was speechless, gulping and sweating.

"Alas! Why are you scared?"

There was silence in the room.

"I will not hurt you."

The room was still silent.

"Haven't you heard of Genie stories? Where does a
Genie grant three boons to a person?"

The room fell silent once more.

"Oh! You are thinking about whether you will be
granted or not. If that's the matter, then don't stress. I will
give you three boons but with two conditions."

Rahul's voice broke the silence, "What's that?" he asked
slowly.

The genie made an expressionless face and stared at
Rahul for a few seconds, "Selfish fellow," the genie said.
"Anyway, the first condition is to treat me like your
friend. Don't make me feel like a genie, make me your
best buddy."

"And the second one?" Rahul asked, to which the genie
once again made an expressionless face and stared at
Rahul for a few seconds. "The second condition is that I
can't grant all three wishes at once. After a few days or
weeks, I will grant other boons."

Rahul readjusted the seat and took a deep breath. The
genie raised his hands above, and a bottle of water
appeared, which he offered to Rahul. Rahul was a bit
relaxed now.

"Beautiful house, man. I'm stunned," the genie said,
looking around. "Hey, have you thought about your first
boon?" Rahul nodded. "What's that? Tell me."

"I have immense money. One thing that money can't buy
is what I will ask for. I'm terrified of pain. So, makes me
congenitally insensitive to pain. Grant me a boon that I

can't feel any type of pain...Can you?" Rahul said with conviction.

"Granted," the genie immediately replied.

"What? Really, how can you be so fast? That's impossible," Rahul voiced with hesitation and a smirk. The genie took Rahul's hand, opened his palm, and a pin appeared.

"What are you mad?"

The genie jabbed him with the pin. Rahul screamed but then realized he couldn't feel the pain.

"We will meet soon, buddy, for your next boon." The genie disappeared.

Rahul sat alone, filled with delight and laughing. But he realized, was it true or was it because of the genie's pin? To confirm his doubt, he took the dumbbell placed beside him, closed his eyes, and on a count of three, threw it on his foot. He was insensitive to the pain. He vigorously laughed and went back to sleep.

That night, he had a dream where Arpita was on her deathbed, and before taking her last breath, she said, "Why don't you ask the genie to cure my cancer?"

Rahul woke up with a fright, sweating. He looked by his side and saw Arpita sleeping peacefully. "Oh, it was a dream!" Rahul exhaled and murmured. "But...I can do that. I can ask the genie for this boon. Arpita will be normal then." Rahul prepared his second boon.

One day, when the couple was back home from dinner, they heard the sound of an explosion, similar to what

Rahul heard that night. They both came out from the parking to see what was the matter, and the explosion sound was replaced by a chaotic noise of people. They saw the building's fifth floor was wrapped in fire. The flames were so gigantic they had never seen before. An immediate rescue and evacuation was started.

A few minutes later, another couple arrived from a party. After seeing the horrific accident, they were broken and tearful. They were rushing here and there, to the firemen, as their house was on the fifth floor where their three children were in the house. By now, the fire had spread widely, and seeing their condition, Rahul decided to rescue the kids. Rahul escaped from there so that he could secretly go inside from another gate. He went up the stairs, and the fire was vividly spread out. As he reached the fourth floor, he saw that the fifth floor was completely submerged in the fire, and the chances of the survival of those kids were bare minimum. Even so, because he couldn't feel pain, he decided to check the apartment once.

There, between huge flames, he saw three kids hiding under a concrete table in terrible condition, shouting for help, struggling for oxygen. He removed his half-burned jacket and stained all three of them in it, grabbing them tightly. He ran from the apartment, reached the third floor, and took them out. His condition was critical. He could see his burned body but couldn't feel the pain. He successfully saved the lives of three children by risking his own, and his boon contributed greatly to this act of bravery.

Rahul was admitted to the hospital and was undergoing treatment. One night, when he was sleeping, the genie appeared in his dream and said gently, "Well done, gentleman. I'm proud of you. Open your eyes and ask for your second boon." The genie was there standing along with Rahul, looking at him, observing him while he was watching the genie in his dream. Rahul still didn't wake up, so the genie peeled one of his burned skins to make him awake, but nothing happened. He forgot that he couldn't feel the pain, so he shouted, and finally, Rahul woke up.

"You are insane, my friend," Rahul said.

"I know."

Both laughed. "So, what's your second wish?" the genie asked.

"Hundreds of years have passed, but no one has found the solution to this. I don't know whether it's possible for you or not," Rahul uttered quietly.

"What's that?" the genie asked immediately.

"Cancer," Rahul's voice broke. "Cure my wife's cancer."

"Done...Your wife has successfully overcome cancer," the genie replied with affirmation.

The genie disappeared.

"Where are you? Where have you gone? My wife is now cured?" Rahul shouted. No genie appeared, but only nurses and doctors.

The next day, to check his wife's cancer, he gently asked his wife to go for a checkup, to which his wife agreed. Doctors did all the examinations, took the tissue samples, and got to know a mystery. There was no cancer in her body. It was disappeared as if it was never there. Doctors were confused about how this could be possible, so they re-examined, but nothing changed in the results. The cancer was gone. She picked up the phone from her handbag and called her love, her face turned pale.

"Hey, Rahul...my cancer..."

"What happened to your cancer?"

"Doctor said, I'm...I'm cancer-free. The cancer because of which I was going to die in a few weeks...mystically disappeared."

He was shocked for a few seconds, but then this news breathed new life into the moment.
While Rahul was overjoyed, Arpita was lost in this mystery. They both started living happily they shifted their home, sold the penthouse, and bought a bungalow. They have everything they could imagine. The couple was living on cloud nine.

Health and wealth are both in their favor. The only sad part in their lives was also vanished. This beautiful situation made him think of his third boon. He was enveloped with all the luxury, what else he could ask for? He started thinking deeply about his third boon.

Unexpectedly Genie appeared.

"Wassup, my friend" Genie playfully inquired. "What's the reason behind your dull face?
Don't you like me present here?"

"No, that's not like that," Rahul said with a wry smile. "Umm...I am thinking of my third boon, what should I ask for? I have absolutely everything."

"Hm, that's true."

"Yeah! Wait...I have everything but you don't." Rahul said excitedly.
"What do you mean?" Genie asked in confusion.

"Every genie has the desire to become human, to live a normal life, and that's my third wish. It's for you, my friend." Rahul replied with conviction. "Can you? Can you become human?"

"Thank you." Genie expressed himself with emotional warmth and happiness. "Before becoming human, I am empowered to grant you one more boon. Ask for anything."

Having all he could imagine, he began to ponder what else he could request. He began to self-reflect and realized he had everything except...Immortality. He wants to be immortal, so he asked.

"I want to be...Immortal. I have everything but still, I couldn't deny death and that's my final boon. I want to be immortal." He declared with a hint of arrogance and a smile.

"It's impossible for me to grant immortality. I can provide anything else—billions of dollars, a cure for any disease, any special power you wish for. Just name it, and I will make it happen, except for...Immortality." Genie spoke with a touch of urgency.

"But you can do anything, why can't this?"
"Because it's a part of the human cycle. I can't."

"Ok, if you can't grant me immortality, then grant me

the boon that...I die from a man, who
is waiting for his end. I die from a man who himself lies
on his deathbed. I die from a man who will follow me to
the grave within minutes." Rahul then made these
conditions to which Genie agreed but didn't feel like it.
Genie wished him luck and disappeared.

Genie was now transformed into a human, he started
working in a cafe. One night, he had a shocking dream,
about the god of death...Yama's shadow was in his
dream, extremely angry, the shadow had only red eyes,
shadow showed signs of intense anger. Yama's shadow
declared with rage, "No one can be immortal and you
have granted him close to immortality, you have to make
him die and you too have to pay the price. "You will be
that person who will kill him, and soon after, you will
meet your end. You will kill your dearest friend and then
join him in death. Life for both of you is only till
tomorrow...Kill him tomorrow.

The next day his stomach started aching, he remembered
his dream, he knew he was going to die in a few hours,
and he was lying on his deathbed. He called his friend
Rahul and asked him to visit his home as he was not
well. He took a dagger in his hand and hid it under the
sheet, Rahul came to his house to check his friend's
condition. As he entered he saw his friend in critical
condition, he sat beside his friend. He said to Rahul that
he could die at any moment, he was trying to tell Rahul
that he was the one who would be the reason behind his
death. The moment arrived, he took out the dagger and
stabbed Rahul multiple times. There was blood
everywhere, the room turned into a pool of blood. Rahul
was dead. The very next

moment his friend was also no longer alive. Both were
dead. His boon turned out to be true. Both together

become the cause of each other's death.
Both together went to the grave. Both together did the journey of death.

We Are Unlucky

Hey, I'm a deaf-mute person and a writer. My name is Javed, but I'm like Jack, "Jack of all trades, master of none." I live by one principle: "Do what you love," and that's why I want my hobby to be my profession. Cool, right? No, because I'm Jack, I don't have one hobby. I'm enveloped with hobbies, and the fun part is that they keep changing, so my desired profession changes too.

"Entrepreneur" was what I wanted to become when my hobby was to learn and read books related to the stock market, trading, and startups. For a few months, I was obsessed with entrepreneurship. Thanks to the subtitles in YouTube videos, otherwise, for a person like me, learning all this would be an uphill battle.

Then I was introduced to the camera. "Photographer" became my new profession and hobby. All day, from morning to evening, it was just me, my camera, different angles, and Click! Click! Click! I photographed everything that came my way, even dog poop. It looked interesting with the macro lens. I determined that I would become the best photographer. But sadly, this didn't last long like entrepreneurship, and my camera was soon replaced by a pen.

"Poetry" became my new hobby. Not because I was in love with someone, and I think I never will be because, how will I listen to someone's voice of love echoing for me? Just kidding. Everyone thinks I write poems because either I'm in love or riding a wave of sadness, but that isn't true. My poetry writing went on, and then I thought, why not write bigger pieces, like articles, short stories, or something fictional? So, I tried this as well.

My life is like a road trip with many beautiful stops along the way. I take a break at each of those stops to enjoy the view, without taking any regrets with me on my remaining journey. Yes, people are jealous of me. How can someone live such a happy life despite having no voice? But I don't care; I'm an unstoppable Jack.

Now meet my younger brother, Ali. Ali can't see. Before, I used to think, "We are unlucky" and how unlucky our parents are because their children were born with disabilities, but with time, this misconception flew away. With disability comes compassion from others, which isn't fair. Treat us like others. Communication between us has been a difficult task. I know sign language, but Ali can't see it. If Ali says something, I can't hear it. What a beautiful irony God gave us. For this, I learned Braille and tactile signing. He places his hands on mine to feel the movements and shapes of the signs.

Ali doesn't have eyes but has a lovely voice. He has sung for a long time and is now performing professionally. Ali is not like me. He loves only one thing, one skill, and has one hobby, which is, of course, singing. He considers himself unlucky despite feeling blessed for his melodious voice. I always tell him that we aren't unlucky, nor are our parents. He also has one dream of making a record-breaking music album, but he only sings. To make his dream a reality and ensure he doesn't have any regrets further in his journey, I figured out something. I will write songs for him, and he will sing them. Our cousin Rohan, a sound-producing intern, will do all the audio engineering. I also know photography, which will help to create an eye-catching album cover. With all this planning in mind, I proposed this idea to Ali.

I entered the room and gently touched Ali's shoulder to let him know I was there. Ali stopped humming and smiled.

"Hi, Javed," Ali said, his voice warm. "What's up?"

I took Ali's hands and began to sign, using the familiar touch signals we had developed. I spelled out, "I have an idea for you."

Ali felt the movements. "What idea?" he asked.

I continued signing. "I'll write songs for you. Rohan will do the audio work. We'll make your dream album."

"Really? You'd do that for me?" he signed.

I nodded, squeezing Ali's hands gently. "Yes. We are not unlucky. We can do this together."

Ali's smile grew wider, and he squeezed my hands back. "Thank you, Javed. This means so much to me."

I signed one last message, my fingers forming each letter carefully. "We are a team. We'll make it happen."

"Yes, we will," Ali gave touch signals back. He was glowing.

We sat together, holding hands. We were both excited about the future. I was happy. Ali's smile gave me goosebumps, and his happiness was now the fuel for me to write my best pieces for his album. I messaged Rohan to tell him about our plan, and he agreed.

Everything was smooth sailing, and I started writing songs. It was raining outside, and my brain was flooded with ideas. I was writing, but then I stopped. I felt hollowness inside me. I was taking breaks in between, checking my phone. I was not the same poet now. I realized I was not happily writing. My interest started vanishing from writing. This was the first time I realized being a Jack is not good. If I started something new, thinking that I was Jack, I would destroy all the happiness of my brother that I saw recently on his face. I was clueless.

My principle of doing only what you love and what gives you happiness was now a big question. Writing for my brother is still what I want, but writing was not giving me happiness. For the first time, I chose to do work that I would not be happy doing but wanted to do for my brother. And on this topic, how sometimes you have to change your principles because it gets necessary, and although it's not wrong, I wrote the first song named, "Jack." I wrote this song on a text-to-speech platform so that Ali could listen to what I wrote, and Ali loved it.

Rohan gave the beat to the song, which I don't know how it sounded, but Ali's reaction was that it was something marvelous. We recorded this song, and all I could see was both of their reactions. Their reactions were telling it was something we called a banger.

"Banger" is the next song I wrote. In this, I wrote about our lives and the connection we share. How we are disabled for others but complete for each other, this bond of ours is a complete banger. Rohan told me he kept the vibe of this song emotional. The beats were slow, and Ali's versatile voice was the cherry on top.

"On Top" is the third song of this album, in which I wrote the imagination of mine, that after the success of this album, how we three will be on top of the world. There were three verses in this song. I shared the struggle of our parents in the starting verse, then our album process in the second one, followed by our success in the third verse. The rocking beat was something Rohan made for this one. The main purpose of this song is to pump up people.

"People" is the fourth song. I told listeners how the people of this world are doing wrong with people like us. This is a freestyle song in which I didn't much focus on rhyming. My motive was that the message I wanted to convey should be strong. After completing my writing, I did find that it made me satisfied. This song was my personal favorite from the album.

In the middle of making the album, Ali started feeling pain in his throat. At first, he thought it was just a cold, but it didn't go away. I noticed Ali struggling more each day. Finally, we went to the doctor, and the news hit us like a storm. This statement, "We are unlucky," was now looking true again. Ali had throat cancer. This meant Ali couldn't sing anymore.

Ali was devastated. Singing was his life, his dream. I felt my heart break for my brother. The studio, once filled with Ali's voice, now felt empty and silent. But Rohan and I refused to give up. We decided to use Ali's old recordings to finish the album. We wanted to honor Ali's dream and his beautiful voice, showing the world the talent that could not be silenced by illness. Rohan then did all the engineering of Ali's old recordings and turned them into songs.

Furthermore, without wasting a single minute, we started doing all the necessary work because Ali's condition was getting critical, and I wanted him to see his album go viral. We named the album "Silent Vision" and uploaded it to every listening platform. We got excited as Ali's dream was about to come true. There was satisfaction with doubt, doubt of getting viral. In the first week, we barely got any streams. I felt broken, and even more when Ali asked us with excitement about the streams.

We started an ad campaign to promote our album, but that didn't work either. At this time, I was tense because Ali was in the last stage of his life, and his biggest dream was still loading. Imagine yourself on the deathbed, and your biggest dream, which if fulfilled will give you immense happiness that you will feel a rebirth of yourself, is still pending and not fulfilled. I was pushing all my limits and had sleepless nights so that Ali could get a peaceful death.

Amid all this hustle, one of the very popular Indian influencers heard about our album and our story. We got so excited. He texted us that he listened to our work and would tell his audience about this album.

I started writing a big thank-you message to him, explaining how this gesture meant a lot and also telling him about Ali's condition. But then he texted that he would charge an amount for this "collaboration." This was a collaboration for him. I thought it was going to be a sweet gesture, but I was wrong. I forgot that we are living among the most generous people.

Just like Ali's biggest dream was to launch a viral album, mine was now to make Silent Vision viral and show Ali that he did it. So, I did this "collaboration."

It went crazy overnight. We got a whopping 600k streams, and it was trending everywhere. Finally, the dream didn't come true as we lost Ali. That night when people were going crazy listening to the album, Ali was battling between life and death, and death won. Neither his biggest dream of seeing his album go viral was fulfilled, nor was mine to show Ali that we made it. We were on the Spotify top lists, but it doesn't matter now. We were lost despite winning, and once again, this thought, "We are unlucky," was winning in my mind.

Custody Of The Moon

In the cosmic courtroom, Earth and Mars stand opposite each other, fighting for the custody of the moon. There was a tense atmosphere inside the courtroom, stars were the curious spectators, and the majestic gigantic radiant Sun was sitting in the center as magistrate.

Blue vibrant Earth spoke first, her voice having the power of oceans and the whisper of forests. "Your Honor, the Moon has been my faithful companion for billions of years. Our bond is not just physical, but emotional and cultural. Moon is part of the culture of people on Earth."

Mars red and rigid immediately scoffed, "Your Honor, I acknowledge Earth's long history with the Moon but I must say that times are changing. With my potential for human colonization, the Moon could play a critical role in expanding life beyond Earth. It's not just about holding onto the past; we must think of the future also."

Venus and Mercury sitting as the jury members had a small chat, Mercury whispered to Venus, "Earth is being very possessive, don't you think?" Venus murmured in return, "I don't think so!"
All other planets in the solar system were jury members.

Sun said while interpreting the chat between Venus and Mercury, "Earth how would your ecosystem be affected if the moon were to leave?"

"Your Honor, my ecosystem will collapse, the moon plays a crucial role in the ecosystem, moon's gravitational pull is very crucial for our oceans. Without the Moon, the civilization on Earth will vanish," Earth responded hurriedly and with tension.

Mars's immediate response stunned everyone, "But a new civilization could form on me with the help of the Moon! I could generate an atmosphere and magnetic field with the help of the Moon."

Earth backed Mars with a great question, "How will you prevent the Moon from crashing into your surface? You have a weak gravitational force!"

Mars was speechless but fumbled for words, "Well…I will…We will find a way!"
Jupiter sitting in the jury, laughed massively just like his size after hearing Mars's response.

The eyes of the entire universe were on this courtroom, everyone was waiting for the decision, and asteroids were coming from outside the courtroom, to see what was happening.

Mars once again broke the silence, "I'm the second closest to the Moon after Earth, I understand everything Earth said about the eradication of civilization. So instead we can share the custody, Moon could spend time with both Earth and Mars, benefiting both planets in different ways."

Earth replied, raising its voice, "It doesn't work like that, Mars."

Saturn whispered with a chuckle in Neptune's ear, "It's getting interesting!" While Neptune gave a cold stare to Saturn in return.

The Sun called for order, its solar flares calming the cosmic chatter. The Sun began, its voice carrying across light-years, "As we have not yet reached a verdict, I am instructing all jury members to come to a decision collectively."

The debate started between the jury members–Mercury, Venus, Jupiter, Saturn, Uranus and Neptune. Jupiter was the foreperson leading the jury.

Mercury began the conversation "I've listened to both sides carefully. Earth's arguments about the Moon's impact on its ecosystem are compelling. However, Mars has innovative solutions that could benefit both planets. But the question is, can we compromise? If yes, then it would be great but if no then I would say the Moon should be part of Mars from now."

Venus asked the members with frustration, "I can't understand why Mars is demanding Earth's moon when it already has its two moons Phobos and Deimos orbiting around it."

"Well, we are not here to discuss about this!" Jupiter ordered while maintaining the decorum.

Saturn entered the conversation, "According to me, in the future, the Moon should now be a part of Mars, perhaps this would be right. Yes, Earth's cultural and emotional connection to the Moon is undeniable, but

Mars is offering a vision of future expansion and people on the Earth are also finding a way to colonize Mars."

Neptune disagreed with Saturn and retorted with a spark, "While Mars' vision for the future is ambitious, we must consider the consequences of removing the Moon from Earth. The Moon plays a significant role in stabilizing Earth's climate and tides. We must prioritize the well-being of existing life. So, my decision will be in favor of Earth, the Moon should remain the part of Earth."

"I agree with Neptune. The Moon's current impact on Earth's ecosystem is vital. The immediate impact on Earth cannot be ignored. Yes, people on the Earth want to colonize Mars, but they never want their moon to be a part of Mars." Jupiter said, nodding in agreement, and continued, "So, up until now Mercury is in favor of Mars, while I and Neptune are in favor of Earth."

Uranus gave his valuable thought in the conversation, "It's essential to respect the established bonds that Earth has with the Moon. Mars' technological advancements are promising, but they cannot immediately replace the Moon's current role in Earth's ecosystem. So, I am also in favor of Earth."

"I'm in favor of Mars! I think the Moon should be part of Mars." Saturn announced.

Everyone was waiting for Venus's response. Every planet watched Venus as they eagerly wanted to know what it would say. Then Venus spoke, "It seems that the Moon's established importance to Earth's environment and culture should be considered more valuable than the plans of Mars. We can ask the court to make any suitable asteroid to be the moon of Mars, which completes the requirement of Mars."

"We're on it! This will also be incredibly beneficial for the long-term Mars missions." Jupiter said with a smile, exactly as he'd hoped, and continued, "So, we concluded that the Moon will stay with the Earth as four have voted in favor of Earth and two in favor of Mars."

Everyone in the court was eagerly waiting to know the results. Mars appeared calm, while Earth seemed a bit nervous. Jupiter, the foreperson, stated the result to The Sun.

After this, The Sun loudly announced the results to the universe, which was eagerly waiting. "The custody of the Moon will remain with Earth. This decision acknowledges the Moon's critical role in Earth's ecosystem and cultural significance. Mars, your innovative proposals are valued, and we have decided to designate a suitable asteroid as your Moon, which fulfills all your conditions."

Earth sighed with relief and said "Thank you, Your Honor, and the jury. I promise to continue valuing the Moon and its role in our shared solar system."

The cosmic courtroom was in a mixture of cheers and gasps. The celestial bodies began to drift back to their orbits while the Sun watched over them all as a silent guardian.

The Pain Of Unspoken Love

"What do you think? Does she like me?" Tarun asked his friend while staring at Sonali. His friend replied with a grin, "She smiles after looking at you, so I guess yes!"

Tarun was submerged in her beauty, constantly staring at her. "How beautifully God has created her," he thought. "Look at those eyes, an ocean of wine. Those curvy lips and that beautiful hair. Oh God!"

Shattering the tranquility, his friend nudged him. "Let's go, it's time for the next lecture." Tarun lived in a small city in Punjab and was the kind of guy who lived for cinematic romance. Sonali was in his class; they both were in high school. His feelings for her weren't recent—they had been growing for a long time. There was always a connection between Tarun and Sonali.

While Sonali was an introvert who didn't like to interact much with anyone, she was very comfortable with Tarun. She was among the most stunning girls in their school, and when she talked with Tarun, he was filled with immense happiness.

Everyone in their school knew about Tarun's feelings for Sonali; it was the talk of the town. Only Sonali seemed unaware of this. One day, her friend Ginni confronted her.

"You know, right?" Ginni asked.

"What?" Sonali replied, feigning ignorance.

"About Tarun's feelings. Don't turn away."

Sonali sighed. "Yeah, I know. So what?"

"So what? Seriously?" Ginni's eyes widened in disbelief. "He acts like a mad lover, waiting only for you for the past few years. The whole school knows about his feelings for you, and you're saying 'So what'?"

"Yes, so what?" Sonali's voice rose in frustration. "There's nothing like love; it's an illusion. He's not in love with me. Once he gets a better girl than me, he'll forget about Sonali. Everyone's like that. That's how love works."

Ginni shook her head. "You're blind."

As their high school was coming to an end, they decided to organize a party. Soon, they'd all be leaving the city for their respective undergrad programs. It was a small get-together—six people were there: Tarun with his two friends and Sonali with her two friends. The four friends wanted Tarun and Sonali to be in a relationship, so they decided to use this party to somehow influence Sonali to date Tarun.

They started playing truth or dare, instructing Tarun to choose 'truth' first so they could ask something, and afterward to choose 'dare'. As planned, he did just that. For 'truth', everyone asked the very same predictable question, but this time in front of Sonali.

"Do you genuinely like Sonali?"

There was silence in the room. Everyone looked at Tarun's face, waiting for his reply. It was obvious, but they wanted to hear it in front of Sonali to see her reaction. Looking into Sonali's eyes, Tarun said, "Yes, I genuinely like Sonali. I'm mad, and she's the reason behind my madness. If I'm happy, she's the reason behind my happiness. And if I'm complete, she'll be the reason behind that completeness."

"Oh! How romantic," one of the friends sighed.

Sonali gasped, doubting her assumptions.

The game continued, and as planned, Tarun chose 'dare'. He was unaware of what was coming, imagining the worst possibilities. But what they gave him was something he never expected.

Everyone except Tarun and Sonali stood up and left. As Ginni passed by, she whispered in Tarun's ear, "Confess to her. Tell her everything. That's your dare!"

"What happened? Why are they leaving without saying anything?" Sonali asked hesitantly.

"It's part of the dare they've given me," Tarun replied, avoiding eye contact.

"What's the dare?"

There was silence for a few seconds. Then, Tarun took a deep breath and started speaking.

"Sonali, I love you. And this isn't just for the dare—I genuinely love you. These aren't recent feelings. I've had them for the past 3-4 years. I haven't confessed until now, but since we're moving out of the city soon, I feel I should before it's too late. You know, I used to find small reasons to talk to you, like asking for stationery even though I had my own. Your voice has always given me peace. When I'm with you, I'm the most comfortable version of myself. With time, these feelings only grew. They never vanished. Now, there's no time of day when I don't think about you. I... I love you."

Again, silence covered the room. They both looked at each other, neither speaking for a long moment.

Sonali finally broke the silence. "Are you sure you love me?"

"Yes, Sonali. Of course. Why are you asking?"

"See, Tarun... I respect your feelings, but I'm afraid to get into a relationship."

"Afraid? Of what?"

"Of betrayal. I easily get attached to someone. That's what I'm afraid of. I think love is an illusion, Tarun."

"No, it's not." He held her hands and continued, "Trust me, I will never leave you. This will be your first and last relationship. We'll take this to the end. Trust me."

Sonali's voice softened. "You know, I never talked to any of the boys in school. It was only you. I think I also have a soft corner for you, but I'm not sure. And as I said, I want only one relationship, so I don't want to rush. Can I get some time? Please?"

"Of course," Tarun replied, his heart soaring with hope.

The party came to an end, and they all left. That same night, Ginni texted Tarun to find out what had happened, and he explained everything. Ginni then decided to talk to Sonali.

Ginni: Hey, blind fellow! What happened today?

Sonali: Don't act like you're unaware. He must have told you everything.

Ginni: Hehe, yeah, he did. So, what do you think?

Sonali: Ginni, you know I'm afraid of relationships. I'm clueless.

Ginni: You aren't. In school, I've seen your feelings for him. You like him somewhere, but you're not accepting it. He's genuinely in love. Look at his loyalty—he didn't approach any girl in the past few years. It was always you for him.

Sonali: Come on, let's not talk about love here. Only he knows whether he genuinely loves me or not. But yes, I do have feelings for him. What should I do? What if he leaves me?

Ginni: He won't. I'm sure of it.

Sonali: Give me some time to think. I don't want to rush. Can I have this whole night? I'll tell him tomorrow morning.

Ginni: Okay, take your time, blind fellow!

Sonali didn't sleep that night, torn by doubt about whether she should date Tarun. She had feelings for him but wasn't sure. Finally, as dawn broke, she decided to say yes.

The next morning was probably the best of Tarun's life. Sonali texted him her decision. After reading her message of acceptance, he was stunned—it was a dream come true. Ginni was happy for them too. They arranged another small party, and this time, Sonali wasn't just Tarun's crush anymore. They walked in as a couple.

They enjoyed their time together, knowing that soon their relationship would become long-distance. Tarun was admitted to a college in southern India, while Sonali went to Maharashtra for her undergraduate studies. Despite the distance, their relationship sailed smoothly at first. They were happily living their separate lives, connected by video calls and messages.

On their first anniversary, Tarun surprised Sonali by visiting her college. They celebrated together, both deeply in love. It was the dream life Tarun had always imagined, with Sonali as his girlfriend.

However, this happiness started to fade in their second year. It became increasingly difficult to find time to talk as they both got busier with their studies and campus life. During a college event that Tarun was leading, he didn't text Sonali once. She was understanding at first, assuming he must be busy, but soon this behavior became a habit. Sonali would wait for his texts and replies, but they came less and less frequently.

After enduring this for a while, Sonali decided to confront Tarun about the issue. At first, he deflected, talking about everything but the problem at hand. But Sonali persisted.

"Tell me what's wrong," she said, her voice a mix of concern and frustration. "We can solve it together. Don't feel like you're alone—I'm with you. Tell me what happened."

Sonali was unprepared for what came next. Tarun spoke in a low voice, guilt evident in his tone.

"I don't know what's happening, Sonali. I... I don't enjoy talking to you anymore. My feelings for you are fading away."

Sonali couldn't believe her ears. Memories of everything—from the party to his heartfelt confession— flashed through her mind. She felt broken, shattered, crumbled. This was something she had never imagined.

"I don't know what's happening, Sonali. I'm sorry," Tarun continued, his voice choked with tears.

"I want to talk, but I just don't feel like it. I'm so sorry." Sonali's eyes welled up, her world slowing down around her. For a few minutes, there was only the sound of Tarun's sobs. When Sonali finally found her voice, it was barely a whisper.

"It's not your fault, Tarun," she said, her words heavy with pain. "You never truly loved me. It was merely an affection. Don't apologize—you haven't done anything wrong. It was inevitable, I suppose, because you only liked me. You didn't love me. And that reality just caught up with us today." She paused, gathering strength for her next words. "I hope you find someone you can truly love, Tarun. The real thing, not an illusion." With that, they broke up. Ginni learned about the breakup and apologized to Sonali for convincing her to give the relationship a chance. For a few days, Tarun was overwhelmed with guilt, often crying and skipping college. But gradually, he began to return to his usual self.

After a month, it was as if nothing had happened. Sonali, however, was forever changed. She couldn't move past the breakup, enduring sleepless nights and endless tears. Everyone was shocked to see her in such a state. She cried more than she talked, sobbed more than she breathed. Concerned, Sonali's parents called her back home for a few days, hoping she would feel better, but nothing changed.

Soon, her sleepless nights began to cause serious mental and physical effects. She wasn't eating properly either. Her parents, unaware of what had truly happened to their daughter, even thought she might be possessed, consulting priests in their desperation. But nothing helped.

Eventually, Sonali was admitted to the hospital. Her condition was critical, and though she started eating again, she still couldn't sleep. She experienced hallucinations of Tarun, and her behavior became increasingly erratic. The doctors prescribed sleeping pills to help her rest.

One day, Ginni told Tarun about Sonali's condition. Overwhelmed with guilt and concern, he decided to visit her. He booked tickets immediately and reached the hospital that night. Ginni was there waiting for him and guided him to Sonali's room.

Without telling anyone, that same night, unable to sleep and consumed by her pain, Sonali had taken an overdose of her sleeping pills.

Tarun arrived and opened the door to Sonali's room. He saw her awake but in a terrible state. He rushed towards her, but she raised a weak hand to stop him.

"Stay away," she said, her voice faint and drained of energy.

"I'm sorry, Sonali," Tarun said, tears streaming down his face.

"It's too late, sweetheart," she replied, a sad smile on her lips.

Their eyes locked, both brimming with tears.

Sonali continued, her voice growing weaker. "Look what you've done to me... No, look what my love for you has done to me. You never truly loved me."

"No, Sonali," Tarun interrupted, still sobbing.

"I always thought love was an illusion," she went on. "But it's not. Look at me. How madly I'm in love, and you're the reason behind my madness. Do you remember saying something like that at that party? I do. I ruined my life, Tarun. You were the greatest gift of my life... and now, I think, my biggest mistake."

The room fell silent as they stared at each other; Tarun crying heavily, while Sonali remained eerily calm.

"Look at yourself," she said softly, "and then look at me. I'm not crying anymore. My tears have dried up." She gasped, her eyes starting to close. With her last few breaths, she whispered, "I loved you, Tarun, and this is what you've given me in return. But... I still love you."

As Sonali's eyes closed for the last time, Tarun's cry echoed through the hospital corridors. The realization of what true, unconditional love meant came too late for both of them.

The Other Writer

One morning, Samuel found pages of his diary filled with some paragraphs and needed clarification.

Samuel was a struggling writer, his many books were published in the market, but they could have done better business. He writes a book, publishes it, and then watches no one buy it, this cycle has been the same for the past few years. He made many changes in his writing style but that didn't work either. This consistent setback was ongoing, but now he encountered writer's block too. He was in great anxiety and self-doubt, his motivation to create something fresh had also disappeared.

One day, he forced himself to write something, so he sat at his table, where he used to write, opened his diary, held a pen, and started writing, but soon he realized, he was not getting any idea. But the determination to write something was holding him back, he fell asleep on the table while thinking about an idea. When he woke up the next morning he found the pages of his diary filled with some paragraphs, further reading revealed it was the opening of a story.

He was in complete confusion, who wrote this story? Did anyone come last night in my home? To verify this thought he checked his house thoroughly and found a coffee mug in the sink, looks like someone made a coffee last night. His doubt was proving to be accurate. Further, he checked the CCTV of the house which was above the entrance, and found out something strange, no one had come to his house last night.

He was shocked, in this state of disbelief he went back to his room and sat on the table, holding his head and thinking about all the possibilities, amid this thinking, he once again read the story written in his diary, and found that, the writing style was different from his style. The whole day he was figuring out who it was, from calling his friends to asking neighbors, but he was only getting disappointed. Despite all his efforts, he achieved nothing. It was night already, he was tired, he ate some leftover food, and went to sleep.

The next morning he woke up, sunlight was coming directly on his bed from the window, giving a nice start to the day. He went to the kitchen to make some coffee and alas there was another coffee mug in the sink, just like before. As he sprinted to his room, his heart pounded with fear. He flung open the door to check his diary, sitting on the table. More pages had been filled, extending the story. Once again someone came yesterday night and wrote a story for him, as if he wanted to write something for Samuel, in his writing block, but this was making Samuel scared.

He once again checked the cameras, but found nothing, asked his friends and neighbors but couldn't find the person. He was filled with many questions, who is this person? How is he entering my house? Why he is writing to me? Only that mysterious person can unfold the answers. Samuel decided not to sleep tonight, he wanted to see who is that person. After taking his dinner he sat at his table and started doomscroling, he had a full plan to catch this person today, but soon sleep overtook him, and he slept on the table.

The next morning, he woke up in regret, he saw his diary was not there, and he gasped, his heartbeat was running fast, and he saw his diary lying on his bed. This sight sent shivers down his spine. Till now he was completely terrified. He was clueless about what to do. Out of nowhere, Samuel came up with a brilliant idea. He decided to write a note for the person, in which he will ask all these questions and keep the note on that page till where the story has been written so that when he starts writing again, he finds that. He mentioned in the note that,

```
I read your work, and while you write
very well, I don't know who you are or
why you're doing this. Would you mind
sharing your name with me? If you
truly want to help, we can meet
tomorrow and collaborate. However,
showing up at night is unnerving and
has to stop. I hope you understand.
```

He kept this short note and went back to sleep. When morning came, he woke up and the first thing he did was check his diary, he opened it and saw the story was extended and on the backside of the note, there was a reply as well.

```
Sorry, my friend, but I can't tell you
my name and who I am, but think of me
as your savior friend, I will make
this book a bestseller. And don't get
scared of me I am here for your good,
stay calm, I won't hurt you. By the
way thanks for the compliment.
```

He initially thought to complain to the police but the urge to know more about this man grew inside Samuels's brain, he also wanted his book to be a bestseller as he was struggling for many years. Samuel thought, for the past three days, this person wasn't harming him, he just

came, wrote, and went, maybe he genuinely wanted to
help. So he decided to cooperate.

He started preparing the desk for him before going to
sleep and talking with him through notes has become
common now, every night he used to place the note and
the next morning woke up excitedly to read the reply.
His diary was also filling, the story was also proceeding
well.
One night, as Samuel's routine, he penned another note.

```
I read the new character that you
introduced, it's very good, and this
character also puts some suspense in
the story. From where did you get this
idea? The way the story unfolds and
the unique approach of depicting the
main character's life in reverse is
impressive. I'm eager to see the
childhood part now; I also want to ask
something.
Since we are good friends now, may I
ask your name?
```

The next morning was a bit unusual, the story was not
written further. Moreover, the things on the table were
scattered, as if someone threw them in anger, there were
not one but four mugs in the sink, and the kitchen was
also a mess. And in reply to the note, there was only
only one line.

```
Never ask my name again! Never.
```

Samuel after this terrific scene of his home is shocked,
and the fear of this man once again surrounds him, but

he consoles himself and decides never to ask the name again.

The story was coming to an end. In the story, the main character's life is in reverse, from old age to childhood, and then he realizes that the main character's childhood story was exactly like his. Everything was so similar – the way he acted, his likes and dislikes, even his parents were like Samuel's parents. This pattern of similar things created doubt in Samuel's head, he was in great disbelief. Constantly putting his brain to think how this person knew about my childhood so well? This cannot be a coincidence.

Further, when the story continues, more similarities come out and this creates great fear and doubts in Samuel's head. Who is this person, who knows so well about me, about my childhood? Samuel asks himself.

After reading the story one morning there was an incident penned down in that diary, and upon reading that Samuel was numbed because that same incident happened to him in his childhood but only he knew that, so how can someone else write that? This was something odd. Samuel decided to know about this person by any means possible. He decided not to cooperate more he planned to wake up all night and watch who would come.

He took his dinner later than the usual time. After that he went to his room and started watching a movie, his plan was not to sleep all night, he was eagerly waiting to know who that person was. It was 2 a.m., and his eyes were starting to droop, but he went to the washroom, splashed water on his face, and then began playing some video games. Soon he got bored with the game as well,

so he picked up that diary and started reading the story
again.
It was 4 a.m., and once again he started feeling
sleepy, in the hypnagogic state he went to was his face,
he stood in front of the sink, he was about to open the
tap, but then he heard a voice, he saw his reflection in
front of him inside mirror saying something to him.

"What was the need to wake up, if you keep staying
awake like this to search for me, I will never come, nor
will your best seller be completed", his reflection spoke
in a very low scary voice. He shifted from a hypnagogic
state to full consciousness. He was terrified, his body
trembling, drenched in sweat, and covered in
goosebumps. He can't process what has just happened.
Was that person in the mirror or was that a dream, he
couldn't identify?

It was morning and that terrific incident had left him
speechless, the fear struck him so intensely that it caused
him to develop a fever. He slept the whole day. At night,
after yesterday's incident, he wasn't in the mood to wake
up again, instead, he performed the previous method, to
write a note for him.

You didn't come yesterday. Is it
because I was awake? Was it you
yesterday inside the mirror, or was
that a dream? This story which you are
writing is also coming to an end, can
you please tell me now, who are you? I
know you don't like this question but
after yesterday's incident, I eagerly
want to know who is this person. And
if in return you want me not to
publish this, then that's fine, I

won't. But I want to know who you
are.

The morning arrived, Samuel woke up, he didn't rush
towards the diary, he went to the kitchen, saw the mug in
the sink, he smiled, then he made some coffee for him as
well with no hurry, as he knew that there is a reply inside
the diary and he wants to read that with comfort. He took
his coffee went back to the room, sat on the table,
opened the diary and there it is, the reply of that note. A
smile came on Samuel's face, he began reading the note
while sipping his coffee.

Yes, I didn't come yesterday, because
you were already there. Wherever you
are, I can't come to that place. It's
strange but true. I told you before,
and I'm telling you now, consider me
as your close friend, who wants to
help you in your bad times. This
story, that I was writing for you for
a few weeks, come to an end, hoping
this to be a bestseller.
In the future also, whenever you face
any problem, I will be there. And as
far as last night is concerned, yes I
was there in the mirror, but I was
looking like you.
Samuel, I want you to know that I'm
you and you are me and
WE ARE ONE.

The Firefly's Curse

Ian was standing on the terrace at midnight, deeply lost in his thoughts. He appeared calm from the outside, but chaos was raging within him. He usually came up to the terrace when he felt anxious, but lately, it had become a habit.

Amid his internal battle, he noticed a small light glowing far away, slowly coming closer. He relaxed a bit after seeing the light; for a moment, all his thoughts vanished, and a smile appeared on his face. The light came closer and closer, and eventually, it revealed itself to be a tiny, charming firefly. He gazed at it, astonished by its glow as if the light had vanished away the darkness in his mind.

He extended his hand, and the firefly gently landed on it. He gasped in relief. He felt an irresistible pull toward the firefly, its light driving him wild, making him lose himself in its glow. His eyes were filled with radiance, and at that moment, he fell in love with the tiny, glowing creature.

The firefly flew from his hand and drifted toward his room, Ian was following closely. It landed on the chest of the side table next to his bed. Ian lay down beside it, his eyes fixed on its soft glow. As he stared at the tiny creature, sleep slowly overtook him as if its presence had vanished the chaos in his mind.

The next morning, Ian woke up, desperately searching for the firefly, but it was nowhere to be found. He rushed around the room, searching every corner and even the terrace, but it had disappeared. He was intoxicated by its glow, and his impatience grew. He desperately wanted to see the firefly again, to feel the inebriation of its light once more, to see his love return.

That night, Ian stood on the terrace, excitedly waiting for the firefly. He was in a terrible state, having not eaten all day, constantly seeking the firefly. When it finally fluttered in from the terrace entrance, Ian smiled. He followed the firefly as it flew about, eventually leading him to his room once more. Ian began talking to the firefly, unaware of how strange his actions were. The firefly was simply relaxed on the chest of the side table, while Ian spoke to it as if under a spell, a spell of love and light. Eventually, he fell asleep, relaxed by its presence.

The next day followed a similar pattern. Ian spent the whole day searching for the firefly but couldn't find it. Exhausted and growing more desperate, he finally had his first meal in two days. That night, the firefly returned. He felt complete again, following the firefly wherever it flew.

Night after night, Ian found himself chasing the firefly, drawn into its glow, captivated by its charm. Each evening, he fell deeper in love with it. This strange routine continued for a week.

One night, as Ian eagerly waited, the firefly entered his room and led him to the terrace. Without thinking, he followed it, standing on the edge, his eyes locked on the glowing creature. As the firefly drifted farther away, Ian, desperate to catch it, reached out. In his obsession, he lost his balance and slipped from the terrace wall. Ian lay on the road below, critically injured, moments from death.

As he lay there, the firefly landed on his blood-stained cheek. Then, in an instant, it transformed into a woman, an anonymous more beautiful than anyone he had ever seen in his life.

The woman began speaking softly, "Ian, in your past life, you were Aden. I loved you then, but you betrayed me. You tried to kill me, pushing me from a terrace."

Tears rolled down from her eyes as she continued, "I pledged that in our next life, you would know the pain of unconditional love. That you would lose yourself completely, as I once did. I never imagined it would end like this."

Ian somehow managed to whisper, "I'm sorry... for what I did then. But this love... it felt real."

"Perhaps, in another life, we'll get it right," she whispered as Ian's eyes closed for the last time. She transformed into her firefly form and the world got to know about a painful but true proof that love and karma and light and dark have a place in people's lives.

Echoes Of Hindi Verses

तुझे देख कर चाँद इतना जला कि सुबह सूरज बन गया,
तेरी चमक से तारे गायब हो गए, रात से दिन बन गया,
फ़रिश्ते तन्हा रहते हैं ये सोचकर कि हिफ़ाज़त कैसे करें तेरी,
क्या जादुई बदन है तेरा, कांटे को छुआ और वो गुलाब बन
गया।

तेरी खूबसूरती के बारे में इतना लिखा,
कि मेरे क़लम को भी तुझसे मिलने की तलब हो गई,
सुंदरी-ए-जादूगर, ऐसा क्या जादू है तेरे हुस्न में,
कि तेरी खूबसूरती की वजह से मेरी स्याही लबालब हो गई।

गुनाह किया है मेरी आँखों ने उसे देख कर,
अब उसकी एक झलक का क़ैदी बन चुका हूँ।

एक आवाज़ सुनी मैंने,
कह रही थी,
मुझे सुकून मिलने वाला है।
मैं खुश हुआ,
और सुकून से बैठ गया,
उस सुकून के इंतज़ार में।

रूखी थी ज़िन्दगी तन्हा चावलों की तरह थाली मैं,
फिर इश्क़ की तरकरी ने रंगीन हर एक दाना कर दिया।

कभी जिन्हे दुख सुनाया करते थे, आज उनसे ही दुखी हें ।

कलम को नहीं खबर,
उसकी स्याही से क्या लिखा जाएगा,
कलम बेख़बर रहता है इस बात से,
कि उसे लिखी लिखाई को याद किया जाएगा।

कुछ भी लिख सकता है वो,
जिसके हाथ में कलम हो,
क्या ही बे-तख़्लीक़ की बीमारी होगी उससे,
जिसके लिए कलम ही मरहम हो।

प्यार के ख़त भी लिखता है ये,
खूबसूरत किताबें भी,
नायाब शेर भी लिखता है ये,
उम्दा ग़ज़लें भी।

ख़यालों को किताबों पर उतारता है,
लिखता है दर्द को भी,
ताक़त भी है काफ़ी कलम में,
लिखता है किसी की मौत को भी।

अगर बात करें मेरे कलम की,
उसे यक़ीनन पता है क्या लिखना है,
एक ही तो हसीना के बारे में लिखता हूँ।
कलम को भी तेरे ही बारे में लिखना है।

इतना लिखा है तेरे बारे में,
मेरे कलम को तुझसे मिलने की तलब हो गई,
ऐसा क्या जादू है तेरे हुस्न में,
तेरी ख़ूबसूरती की वजह से मेरी स्याही लबालब हो गई।

आज फिर दुखी हुआ हूँ मैं
आज फिर टूटा हुआ हूँ मैं
हर चीज़ सलामत थी शाम तक
रात में आज फिर अकेला हुआ हूँ मैं।

कभी तरसते थे जिसको देखने के लिए सुबह शाम,
आज उसी को देख कर अनदेखा कर देते हैं।

आज कलम भरा है लफ़्ज़ों से,
लिखने को बेसब्र है,
देखा होगा वापिस उसको,
ये अल्फ़ाज़ उसी के तो असर हैं।

उसने कभी खिलता गुलाब दिया था,
कभी अपना वक्त दिया था,
खुश करने के लिए मुस्कान दी थी,
सोने के लिए अपना ख्वाब दिया था।
तोहफा भी दिया था उसने कभी,
कभी उसने नूर दिया था
डूब जाने को उसने आंखें दी थीं,
इबादत के लिए अपना प्यार दिया था।

इन बिखरे हुए पलो में, बिखरा हुआ मैं,
कोशिश कर रहा हूँ समेट जाने की
लड़खड़ा रहे हैं जो सबात-ए-ख़याल मेरे,
कोशिश कर रहा हूँ इन्हें मजबूत बनाने की।

एक दिन अकेला लेटा था बिस्तर पर,
किसी को बाँहों में भरने का मन था,
नींद भी नहीं थी आँखों में,
किसी को गले लगाने का मन था।

बस तकिया और था बिस्तर पर,
उसी को भरा फिर बाँहों में,
इतनी खूबसूरत झप्पी दी उसने,
कभी ना सोची थी ख्वाबों में।

ऐसा लगा मानो,
सब मुकम्मल हो गया,
मेरा किसी को बाँहों में भरना,
भी पूरा हो गया।

और कस के पकड़ा तकिये को,
डर था कहीं भाग न जाए,
और कस के पकड़ा तकिये को,
ताकि अकेलापन मेरा सारा मिट जाए।

फिर तकिये से एक सवाल पूछा,
कहाँ था तू इतने दिनों से?
गले लगाने को जब चाहिए था मुझे कोई,
कहाँ था तू इतने दिनों से?

हर रात तेरे सिर के पीछे,
हमेशा तेरे साथ था,
लेकिन तुझे आस थी महबूब की,
मुझे भूल कर तू उनके पास था।

अब सिर के नीचे रखने से ज़्यादा
तकिया मेरी बाँहों में होता है,

नींद भी खूबसूरत बन गई है मेरी,
क्योंकि तकिया मुझे अब गले लगाकर सोता है।

तू ख्वाबों की अप्सरा, एक नायाब सी मुराद,
मिल जाए जिसे भी, वो खुशियों से आबाद।
जाम भरी आँखें, हर कोई देखने को बेताब,
गुलाबी हैं होंठ, सुनहरी हैं जुल्फ़ें, खूबसूरती है बरकरार।
सादगी से भरी, तेरा हुस्न बेशुमार,
और मोहब्बत से भरा मेरा दिल बेकरार।
तू ख्वाबों की अप्सरा, एक नायाब सी मुराद,
मिल जाए जिसे भी, वो खुशियों से आबाद।

परींदा की तरह आज़ाद हो तुम
अजब सी कोई दास्तां हो तुम
रूप फरिश्ते जैसा है तुम्हारा
इबादत में माँगने वाला ख्वाब हो तुम
दीवानों की नायाब दीवानगी हो तुम
हसीन रूप, खूबसूरती की मिसाल हो तुम
इत्मीनान से देखने वाला गुलाब हो तुम
सादगी से भरी हुई मिठास हो तुम
सिर्फ एक गाना वक़्फ़ नहीं कर सकता तुम्हें
कई खूबसूरत गानों का भंडार हो तुम
मधुर संगीत जो कोयल गाए
वैसी कोयल की मीठी राग हो तुम
मस्ती-ए-खुशबू में झूम उठूं मैं
ऐसी खुशबू का आगाज़ हो तुम
परिधि हो तुम, खुशियों से भरे दायरे की
मस्ती भरी एक परी नायाब हो तुम

End Word

This is my first book. While writing the poems and stories you've just read, I never imagined I would publish them. I write because I discovered my world through words, and I hope you find your own world within them. What began as a hobby a year ago has now turned into this—a collection in your hands, crafted by a novice wordsmith. I hope you enjoyed it.

About the writer

Having started his writing journey in high school, he tries to craft impactful narratives. Beyond his pen, he explores humanity through dialogue, capturing ideas. He believes that imaginative ideas find beauty in detail.

You can contact him on

tanishq.k.kalra@gmail.com
https://www.instagram.com/_tanishqkalra_

9 798889 556671